Family Devotions
FOR THE
Advent Season

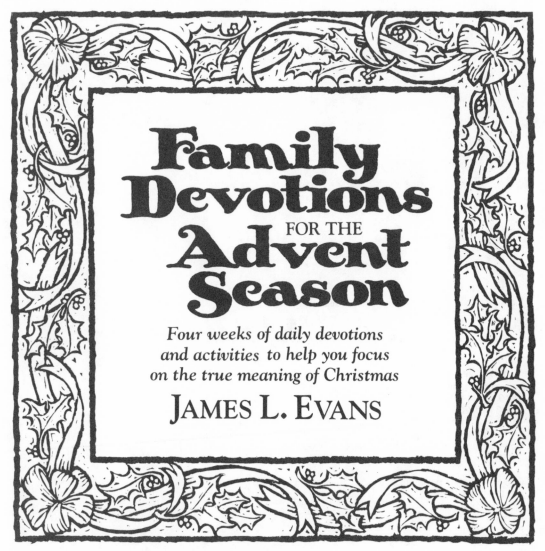

Family Devotions
FOR THE
Advent Season

*Four weeks of daily devotions
and activities to help you focus
on the true meaning of Christmas*

JAMES L. EVANS

TYNDALE HOUSE PUBLISHERS, INC.   WHEATON, ILLINOIS

Library of Congress Cataloging-in-Publication Data

Evans, James L., date
    Family devotions for the Advent season / by James L. Evans.
        p.   cm.
    ISBN 0-8423-0865-2
    1. Advent—Prayer-books and devotions—English.   2. Family—Prayer-
books and devotions—English.   I. Title.
BV40.E83   1991
242′.33—dc20   91-65584

Cover and interior illustrations copyright
© 1991 by Jean Arnold

For
April, Christy, Bethany, and Jeremy
who remind me daily
that we enter the kingdom as children

CONTENTS

The Meaning of the Advent Season

N early every Christmas season I hear someone pray: "Lord, help us to keep Christ in our celebration of Christmas." Behind that concern is the realization that the day set aside to celebrate the birth of our Savior has become highly commercialized and in some cases fully exploited for the sake of profit.

The celebration of Christmas is an act of worship carried out by the Christian community. When the celebration becomes something other than worship, it is also something other than Christmas. Allowing any part of the Christian gospel to be mixed with cultural, national, or social images runs the risk of distorting the meaning of the gospel.

The danger with so many competing and conflicting images surrounding the modern celebration of Christmas is that we let the true meaning slip away from us. This is especially true for children who have to deal with huge amounts of conflicting information. In an interview recently, children in a shopping mall were asked, "What is the meaning of Christmas?" Their replies included Santa Claus, Christmas presents, trees, and bright lights. One little fellow even said, "I think it has something to do with the discovery of America"!

Of course, children learn about Christmas, as they do about most things, from their families. Helping families, therefore, develop strong and meaningful understandings about worship in general and Christmas in particular is crucial to keeping the distinctive truths of Christianity alive.

One way our family has tried to keep the meaning of Christmas focused on the gift of the Savior (rather than the gifts under the tree!) is by using the Advent wreath.

THE MEANING OF ADVENT

The word *advent* comes from the Latin *adventus* and means "coming." Celebrating the Advent season means celebrating the coming of Jesus as God's gift to the world. Churches in the liturgical tradition observe the four weeks preceding Christmas Day as part of their Advent celebration. Each week symbolizes a different aspect in the story of Christ's coming.

Many interpretations exist for the four symbols. This is the way we understand the weeks of Advent.

The first week remembers the prophets. During this week, worship focuses on how long the world waited for the arrival of God's Messiah.

The second week focuses on God's preparation. Worship is built around the different people God used to prepare the way for the coming of his Son.

The third week considers our response. We are challenged to reflect on all that God has done and respond to his gracious act in love and faith.

The fourth week emphasizes God's love. Here we are invited to celebrate the great love of God that makes life and eternal life possible.

The Advent wreath is used to help symbolize and visualize the meaning of these four divisions. The wreath is decorated with five candles. The weeks are marked by the lighting and burning of a candle during the worship service.

The first three weeks are symbolized by dark purple candles. These symbolize the darkness of the world before the arrival of the Messiah. The fourth candle, used during the week of love, is pink. It stands in contrast to the dark candles and symbolizes our hope.

In the center of the four candles stands one large white candle. This is the Christ candle. We light this candle on Christmas Day along with the other four. The candles burning together, with the Christ candle in the center, symbolize God's act of sending light into our world of darkness.

The symbolism of the wreath is also important. Greenery represents life and the gift of life. God creates life through his loving grace. He also redeems life through the same grace. The wreath is a picture of God in all of his creative activities on our behalf.

Using the wreath in home worship is very simple. An Advent wreath can be easily and inexpensively constructed. Using two pieces of wood or heavy cardboard, fit them into the shape of a cross. This will serve as the frame. Use lightweight string or wire to secure real or plastic greenery in a circle around the frame. Holly or pine boughs can be used as greenery. Then you attach plastic or glass candle holders to the points of the cross. Affix a larger holder for the central candle in the middle of the wreath.

Most florists make or stock wreaths that can be adapted for this special purpose. Some even prepare Advent wreaths for churches and could easily prepare smaller ones for use at home.

HOW TO USE THIS BOOK

Using this worship guide along with the wreath is also easy and can be quite meaningful. Each day, at an appointed time, a candle is lit, Scripture is read, and the meaning of that particular candle is discussed. The first Sunday of Advent is the Sunday nearest November 30. However, the Advent season actually begins four full weeks before Christmas Day. Therefore, this worship guide is designed to be used beginning on November 27.

If your church observes the Sundays of Advent, you may find that the Sundays do not exactly coincide with the divisions in the book. By Christmas day, however, you will catch up.

The activities in this book are aimed at families with younger children. However, the Scripture and themes can be altered or recast so that both youth and adults can enter fully into the meaning for each day.

Daily Format

- Scripture reading for the day.

- Brief description of materials needed to gain children's interest. Look over these in advance to be sure you have the supplies on hand. Most of the activities call for items that are present in virtually every home.

- Description of how to use the materials and how to relate them to the thought for that day. Read this over carefully in advance. Ideally, the worship book should not even be present at your worship time. The Bible, your wreath, and the burning candles are enough. Read the instructions over carefully so that you can lead the activity without referring back to the book.

- Prayer focusing on the theme of the lesson.

- Discussion questions that enhance family participation and encourage everyone to apply the lesson to his or her own life.

- An assignment to reinforce the theme of the lesson.

You may have a question about which Bible to use. Several versions were consulted in preparing the lessons. A modern translation helps children hear the Scriptures in everyday language. Translations that are very good for children include *The Living Bible* (TLB), the New International Version (NIV), the *New American Standard Bible* (NASB), and Today's English Version (TEV).

A NOTE ON TEACHING CHILDREN

Children love to *do*. They are "hands on" learners. Allow your child(ren) to do as much as possible so that the experience will be a real family worship activity. If possible, allow the children to actually read the Scripture passage for each day's worship time. If your child is too young to read, let him or her light the candle.[1] If you have more than one child, let them share responsibilities—one light the candle, one read Scripture, and so forth. Children always get more out of an activity where they participate. The worship guide has suggestions for how to accomplish this.

Preparation

It's important to create a worshipful atmosphere. You can do this by talking about this new way of celebrating Christmas several days before actually beginning. Establish a regu-

---

1 Be sure to caution children that the candles are only to be lit during the worship time and only with an adult present.

lar time. Since the effect of the candles is greatly enhanced by reduced light, an evening time might be preferred.

Allow plenty of time for each worship activity. Try to find a time where you do not feel pressed to hurry because of bedtime or a favorite television program. Allow enough time for everyone to experience the joy and power of the message of Christmas.

The final worship activity is for Christmas Day. If your children are like mine, the first thing they say on Christmas morning is, "Where are the presents?" Let children be children. It may be wise to let them enjoy the time of seeing what is under the tree. After breakfast, or later in the day, bring the Advent season to a close by participating in the final exercise. This way, the final family emphasis will not be "What did we get?" but rather, "Look what God has given!"

The word *Christmas* literally means "Christ-worship." It comes from the Middle English expression *Christemasse*. My hope and prayer is that this guide will contribute to finding an answer to our prayer: "Lord, help us to keep Christ in Christmas." After all, if Christ is not in our Christmas, then it is not really "Christ-Mas," is it?

Waiting for the Lord
FIRST WEEK OF ADVENT
November 27 to December 3

The people of Israel experienced two serious disappointments in their long history. These disappointments led them to hope and believe that God would send his Messiah, a Chosen One, to make things right.

The first disappointment concerned Israel's kings. After the time of David and Solomon, very few of the kings in Israel measured up to God's ideal. Many of the prophets saw in this human failure the need for a divine kingship. Through the inspiration of the Holy Spirit, they proclaimed that a special king sent directly from God would soon appear. God's king would rule with justice and compassion. This king would not disappoint the people or God.

The second great disappointment came when the people of Israel were taken into captivity. Separated from their homeland, their temple, and their dreams, the people felt their hope slipping away. From the enemy soil of Babylon and Assyria, however, the prophets continued to proclaim God's plan for the future. The bold and courageous words of Jeremiah, Isaiah, and Ezekiel, kept the embers of hope alive in the despairing exiles. They were given hope. But, they were told to wait. God's time was not their time, and so they waited and longed for Messiah—their special king—to appear.

During this week, you will be lighting one purple candle—known as the "Prophets' candle." Try to imagine the eager waiting and longing for the appearance of God's chosen One. Lead your family to make a commitment to a week of waiting—waiting for the Lord.

NOVEMBER **27**

Light First Purple Candle

Waiting for a New Covenant

SCRIPTURE
READING

Jeremiah 31:31-34

MATERIALS
NEEDED

Two photographs of an adult member of the family. One photo should be of the person as a child. The second should be a more recent picture.

LESSON

Light one purple candle. If you have a child old enough to read, ask him or her to read aloud the verses for today. When the Bible reading is finished, ask: "What is a covenant? Why do you think God was going to make a new covenant?" After answers are given, explain that a "covenant" is like a very serious promise. It's a bargain, a contract.

Show the two pictures side by side. Say something like, "This is an old picture and a new picture. They are of the same person, but they are different. In one, the person is young; in the other, he/she is grown.

"God's covenant was his promise to always take care of

his children, Israel. And Israel's responsibility was to trust in God and obey him. The covenant was written on stone and given to Moses. By the time of Jeremiah, people were not taking God's covenant seriously. They were not obeying God—they were not holding up their end of the bargain.

"So God promised a *new* covenant: not a different one, but a 'grown-up' covenant, an improved one. The new covenant was to be written on people's hearts instead of on stone." Ask: "How did God keep his promise about a new covenant?" (By sending Jesus as Messiah.)

"Jeremiah said that 'the days are coming. . . .' The people of Israel knew this meant that they would have to wait for the new covenant."

DISCUSSION "When is it hard to wait?" Allow children an opportunity to answer. "What makes waiting difficult?" After they answer, say, "As we wait to celebrate the birth of God's Son, we learn to appreciate the importance of waiting on God. Sometimes we may wonder when he will answer our prayers. But we must keep praying and wait for him. We understand how God's people waited for the New Covenant."

PRAYER Invite all family members to pray, thanking God for the New Covenant in Jesus.

ASSIGNMENT   Ask everyone to think of at least two times they have waited on God (for example, an answer to prayer). Children may need help in thinking of different events they have waited for. Encourage everyone to share their thoughts tomorrow night.

Light First Purple Candle

Waiting for Justice

SCRIPTURE
READING

Isaiah 11:1-4a

MATERIALS
NEEDED

A sports rule book (such as used in softball or football) or a list of rules from a favorite board game. Class rules or playground guidelines can also be adapted for this activity.

LESSON

Have everyone report on the assignment from last night. Then light the first purple candle again. Have someone read the Scripture verses aloud. Show the rule book or list of rules. Say something like, "Imagine that we are playing a game, and every time you start winning I change the rules so you start losing. How would that make you feel?" (Possible answers could include: angry, sad, hurt, frustrated.) "When we play a game with others, we expect them to obey the rules and play fairly. The Bible also talks about fairness. The word often used is *justice*. Justice means doing things right and making things right. It means playing by God's rules.

"In the days of Isaiah the prophet, almost no one was playing by the rules. People in government cheated and took things that belonged to others. Even people who were in charge of worship in the temple could not be trusted. People who bought and sold the food and animals raised by the poor were often dishonest and took advantage of their customers by giving them less money than the goods were worth.

"Because of this unfairness, many people were angry and disappointed. They wanted fairness, justice. Isaiah was talking to them in these verses. He promised that God had not forgotten them: God would send them a King who would make sure that justice would be practiced by all people."

DISCUSSION

"What examples are there of unfairness today?" (Possible answers would include: people who cheat others out of money, leaders who do not care for people as they should, teachers who grade unfairly, etc.) "How do you think God feels about people who do not play by the rules? What does he want them to do?"

After everyone has had a chance to answer, say: "The promise of a new King was good news for the troubled people of Isaiah's day. They knew God would help them. But first, they had to wait. God's plan would take time. They knew that God's help was coming, but not right away. They were waiting for the justice that Jesus, the Messiah, would bring."

PRAYER

Lead your family in prayer, asking God to help people in our world who may be victims of injustice. Also ask the Lord to help you and your family to always be fair in your dealings and, as you wait for Christmas Day, to grow in compassion.

ASSIGNMENT

Before the next lesson, play a simple board game together—do a couple rounds, first without any rules. Then play the game again, with the rules.

Waiting for the Hurt to Stop

SCRIPTURE
READING

Isaiah 40:1-5

MATERIALS
NEEDED

Items from a first-aid kit: ice pack, bandages, Band-Aids, aspirin, and so forth.

LESSON

Light the first purple candle again. Have someone read the Bible passage aloud. Then begin by describing how painful an injury can be. (If someone in the family has suffered a painful injury, use that person's experience as an illustration. Otherwise, encourage everyone to use their imaginations about how it might feel to hurt.)

Display the first-aid items. Say something like, "When we are hurting, the first thing we want to do is stop the hurt! We might use items like these to help us.

"Sometimes hurt is on the inside. This is the kind of hurt that comes from being afraid or being lonely. The children of Israel hurt because they were away from their homes and land.

"You see, long ago, 587 years before Christ was born, the powerful nation of Babylon defeated Israel and took many of the Israelites back with them to Babylon to work as slaves. The children of Israel were forced to leave their homes and farms and live in a foreign land. They were held against their will for over 70 years.

"During this time, they suffered great pain." Ask: "What kind of pain do think they felt while away from home?" (Help children understand that not only were they "home-sick," which is a kind of pain, but they were also mistreated. It is not possible to hold a people in slavery without humiliating them.) Allow time for everyone to respond.

"The message of the prophet Isaiah was given to the people of Israel to assure them that God was aware of their hurting. He would help them and stop the pain.

"The people of Israel believed Isaiah's message. His words were a source of comfort to them while they waited for the hurt to stop. Eventually, they were allowed to return home. They knew that God would also keep his word about sending the Messiah. They knew that once God's Son came, all of the hurting would be over."

DISCUSSION

Ask everyone to think for a moment of how people in our world may be hurting. "What are some of the things that hurt people? Do you think God can still stop the hurt?" Allow time for answers.

PRAYER

Lead your family in prayer, asking God to help the hurting people. Pray also that as you wait for Christmas Day, that you will grow in gratitude for all that God has done for you.

ASSIGNMENT

Give everyone a postcard and a pen. Tell them to write a note of encouragement to someone they know who may be hurting. They could thank a person for something, assure a person of their love and prayers, offer congratulations, or just send special greetings. Help younger children compose the note and then write it for them. Another option would be to make a family card to send to someone who is hurting.

Waiting for the Music

SCRIPTURE
READING

Isaiah 51:1-5

MATERIALS
NEEDED

Anything musical. If musical instruments are available, use them. Otherwise a radio, tape player, or record player will work very well.

LESSON

Light the first purple candle again. Have someone read the Bible verses aloud. Then suggest to the family that you listen to a little Christmas music. Explain that music is an important part of life and allow everyone to name their favorite song. Sing one of the family favorites together.

Afterward, say something like, "Imagine how sad it would be if there was no music in our world. Or worse, just as we were enjoying our music, it suddenly stopped. Just think how sad it would be if we thought we would never hear singing again.

"The children of Israel loved to sing. They sang songs about God's love for them. They sang songs about God's rescue of the people from Egypt in the days of Moses. They sang songs about the mighty acts of God throughout history.

"When the Babylonians took them away from their homes and from their temple, they did not feel like singing anymore. The music stopped because they did not think they could sing songs about God in a foreign land." (Turn to Psalm 137 and read the first four verses.)

"The prophet Isaiah knew how important music and singing was to them. He knew that when they returned home, it would be a day of celebrating and singing. The sound of music would return.

"But first, they had to wait. The music in the temple had been stilled, but not forever. While they were waiting, they could still worship. Help was coming. God was sending his King, and renewed singing would mark his arrival!"

DISCUSSION

"What kind of music would we play or sing when we're happy? When we're sad? How can music help our feelings? Teach us? How can we worship God through music?" Allow time for everyone to answer.

PRAYER

Lead your family in prayer, thanking God for the beauty of music. Close by singing a special Christmas song together.

ASSIGNMENT

Instead of watching TV tonight, play Christmas music.

Waiting for a Shepherd

SCRIPTURE
READING

Isaiah 53:1-12

MATERIALS
NEEDED

Paper and crayons or pencils. You will be asking everyone to draw a picture of sheep and a shepherd. If you have a set of encyclopedias, you may want to look up "sheep" and "shepherding." If there are good pictures, you may want to use them instead of the drawings.

LESSON

Light the first purple candle again. Have a family member read the Scripture passage. Afterward, reread verse six.

Get everyone started on their drawings if that is what you are doing. After a few moments of drawing, ask why sheep need a shepherd. Encourage children to use their imaginations as they answer. Allow a few moments for responses, and be sure to affirm their answers.

When the children begin to run out of ideas, describe the importance of the shepherd to the sheep. The shepherd was responsible for finding grazing lands and fresh water for his sheep. If threatening weather arose, the shepherd would lead the sheep to a safe place to wait out the storm. Often wild animals—wolves and lions—would follow the sheep in order to capture strays. The shepherd was always on guard to fight off such attacks and save the sheep from harm. Sometimes a faithful shepherd would be injured or killed defending his sheep.

"Why do you think the prophet Isaiah told the people of Israel that God would send someone who would give his life for them?

"The people of Israel felt afraid and threatened while they were in Babylon. They were far from home. They were afraid their captors might harm them. They felt scattered and weak. Isaiah said they were like sheep. He also said that God's promised King would be like a shepherd who lays down his life in order to save the sheep. The King or Messiah would suffer and die so that his people could be saved.

"Isaiah promised that at the right time, their King, the Good Shepherd, would come and lead his sheep to safety. People are lost today, like straying sheep. They need to be saved—they need the Good Shepherd."

DISCUSSION

Ask everyone to read John 10:11. (Little ones may need an adult or older sibling to help them.) Say something like, "We know now that Jesus is the Good Shepherd. What did

Jesus do to save us, his sheep?" (He died for our sins, taking our place on the cross so that we might have eternal life.) "How does Jesus lead us today, as our Shepherd?" Allow time for answers.

PRAYER

Lead your family in prayer, thanking God for sending Jesus to lead you and guide you. Pray asking God to help you follow where your shepherd leads. Close by reading Psalm 23.

ASSIGNMENT

Put the drawings or the pictures on the table or the refrigerator as a constant reminder that Jesus is our Shepherd and we are his sheep. Have everyone memorize John 10:11. (Older children and adults may want to memorize Psalm 23.)

DECEMBER **2**
Light First Purple Candle

Waiting to Be Saved

SCRIPTURE
READING

Isaiah 52:7-10

MATERIALS
NEEDED

A toy helicopter or a picture of a helicopter, rolls of Life Savers candy.

LESSON

Light the first purple candle again. Have a family member read the passage from Isaiah 52:7-10 aloud. Show the helicopter or the picture of the helicopter and ask: "What would you call this?" Children, of course, will reply "helicopter." Encourage them to think harder. Ask them what else they could call it. Children might reply: flying machine, whirlybird, chopper, and so forth.

After they have exhausted their ideas, say something like, "A helicopter can also be called a 'lifesaver'!" (You may live near a hospital that has "life flight" helicopter ambulance service. Or someone your family knows may have been served by a life-saving helicopter. If so, and the children pick up on that, start there.)

"A helicopter can be used by a hospital as a lifesaver. If someone is injured or very sick and is a great distance from the hospital, the helicopter can get there quickly and fly the person to the doctors.

"Imagine that someone you care about very much needs to get to a doctor quickly. Think of how happy you would feel if suddenly a fast helicopter appeared to rush him or her to the hospital. You would know that your loved one would soon be safe.

"The prophet Isaiah told the people of Israel that a 'life flight' would be coming, not a helicopter, but God's chosen King, his Messiah. Isaiah told them that before long the whole world would see how God could save his people. Isaiah promised Israel that their pain and worry would soon end. Help was on the way."

DISCUSSION

"How do you think the people of Israel felt when they heard that help was coming?" (Glad, happy, excited, relieved.) "Do you think it was difficult for them to wait? Why or why not?" Allow everyone to answer.

Then say, "God's saving power still comes to people. How are people trapped 'in captivity' today? How are they in danger?" After they answer, ask: "How does God rescue them (and us)?"

After the answers, say: "God wants all of his people out of danger. As we wait for Christmas Day, let us pray for those people in our world who need to be rescued. Let's pray that they will hear the good news about God's 'life flight.' Maybe there are some *we* can tell."

PRAYER   Lead your family in prayer for the people who need God's saving power in their lives.

ASSIGNMENT   Give everyone a roll of Life Savers candy. Tell them to carry the roll as a reminder of God's saving power and to pray for a person who needs Christ each time they eat one.

DECEMBER 3

Light First Purple Candle

Waiting for the News

SCRIPTURE
READING

Malachi 3:1

MATERIALS
NEEDED

A daily or weekly newspaper. If this is not available, use a news magazine or even a newsletter from church or school. If none of these are available, you can simply refer to the nightly news on television.

LESSON

Light the first purple candle again. Read Malachi 3:1 aloud. Hold up the newspaper or news magazine and ask the children to identify it. Ask: "Why is news important to us?" Allow everyone an opportunity to answer.

Afterwards say something like, "News is important to us for many reasons. We can know if a storm is coming by reading the weather report. We can know if important meetings are being held at the school or at city hall by keeping up with the daily news.

"Suppose we hear that someone important will be coming to town. Maybe it is someone we really want to meet,

the president of the United States, or a famous sports figure or entertainer. We would learn when he was coming
and where we could see him by keeping up with the news.

"Now imagine our world without news. Try to think
what it would be like never to know what the weather was
going to be like until it was already here, or to never know
that something important was going on until it was already
over. We would really miss not having news.

"Something like this happened to the people of Israel
when they returned from Babylon. God brought them out,
just as he said he would. But it was not time for the new
King to come just yet. So the people were disappointed.
Every day they wondered when God's promised King
would appear.

"About that time, Malachi the prophet began to say to
the people of Israel, 'Be patient. It won't be much longer.
The new King is on the way!'

"The people wanted to know when. 'How much longer
do we have to wait?' they asked.

"Malachi replied, 'I'm not sure how long. But this I do
know. God will make sure the news goes out to you. He
will send a messenger to prepare for the arrival of the King.
You will know when the time is near because the messenger will bring the good news!'

"Today, we know that John the Baptist was the messenger who prepared the way for Jesus' arrival. For the people

of Malachi's day, however, the word was, 'Wait just a little longer.' But their wait would soon be over. The news was about to break—the King was about to arrive!"

DISCUSSION   Look over today's paper together for news of the arrival of an important person somewhere. Discuss how you would feel to read that Jesus was coming. Ask how God has given us the news about Jesus.

PRAYER   Lead your family in prayer, thanking God for taking steps to let the whole world know that the King has indeed been given. Thank him also for keeping his promises.

ASSIGNMENT   Have everyone write an announcement of Jesus' coming that they might give on the television news. They should be prepared to give their news bulletin tomorrow night.

Preparing for the Lord
SECOND WEEK OF ADVENT
December 4 to December 10

Help your children understand the importance of preparation. If they are school age and take tests, preparation in the form of study would be a good illustration. Perhaps your family enjoys camping. You could talk about preparation in terms of planning and stocking up for a camping trip. Preparation can also be illustrated by cooking a meal, putting together a model plane, or planting a garden.

Relate how important preparation was to God in sending Jesus to us. God sent his Son into the world at just the right time, after careful planning and preparation.

It was the right time in history because:

• First-century political and economic situations had created high expectations for the arrival of the new King.

• The widespread use of Greek allowed the gospel story to be made available to the whole world quickly. Greek was as close to a universal language as the world had ever known.

• The numerous safe and well-protected roads paved the way for the apostles to carry the Good News to many nations.

But more important than any of this, God had prepared people by working through the hearts and minds of faithful believers to prepare the way for the appearance of his Son.

This week of activities will focus on some of these special people. Through this study, you and your family will gain an appreciation for God's patient planning.

You also find yourselves in God's plan. In the same way that God prepared people for the arrival of his Son, he still prepares people to embrace the Good News, which is Jesus the Christ. Pray that God will do his work of preparation in you and your family so that you might be ready for the advent of his Son.

During this week you will light two purple candles. The new candle is known as the "Bethlehem candle." It helps focus on the ordering of events and people that led to the birth of Jesus.

SPECIAL NOTE TO SINGLE PARENTS

The first two activities in this week presuppose a family where Mom and Dad are both present. I realize this is not true for many families who may use this book. Let me encourage you to adapt the material to fit your situation. Whether you are single because of the death of a spouse or because of divorce makes little difference to what you are trying to accomplish in terms of worship. The value of "mother" and "father" reflected in the two activities is true. Moms and dads may not always live up to the ideals, but children still need to know what those ideals are. I suspect that our children's high opinion of us may actually serve to make us better parents.

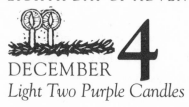

DECEMBER **4**
Light Two Purple Candles

Preparing a Mother

SCRIPTURE
READING

Luke 1:26-38

MATERIALS
NEEDED

Something that symbolizes "Mom" in your family. This symbol will be different for different families. For instance, Mom in your house may be a career woman: doctor, teacher, nurse, business person. You may want to use something from her career as a symbol. These might include: briefcase, stethoscope, grade book, and so forth.

On the other hand, Mom may be at home full time. Therefore, you may want to use a symbol from her work in the home: cooking spoon, sewing materials, the calendar and family schedule she keeps, etc. The point is to provide an object that your children will readily associate with their mother.

LESSON

Have everyone give their "news bulletins," the assignment from last time. Then light two purple candles. Point out that during the second week of your celebration, you will be lighting two candles. Remind everyone of the meaning of the candles for this week: preparation. Have a family member read aloud the Scripture passage for today.

Show the selected object to the family. Say something like, "This represents Mom. Mom is an important part of our family. She does a lot for us. We are very grateful for her and her special gifts to our family.

"God understands the importance of a good mother. That is why he was very careful in his selection of a mother for Jesus. God chose Mary because he knew she would provide the right kind of care and love for his Son.

"Even though Jesus was God's Son, he was also human. As an infant and small child, he needed the same mothering that all children need. God knew that Mary would raise Jesus in a home filled with love.

"Jesus' mother was just as important to him as your mother is to you. She was prepared by God to bring his Son into the world. She was also prepared to care for God's Son and provide for his needs until he was ready to leave home and begin the work that God had given him.

"As we look forward to Christmas Day, don't forget that God prepared a mother. God chose a very special woman to raise his Son. He also prepares all of us to be his children. He prepares us by helping us to understand his purposes in sending his Son.

"Mary is our example of how to respond when God calls. "Say yes!"

DISCUSSION

Ask what God might be calling or asking each of them to do. Answers could include helping someone, being kind to the new kid down the street, having a good attitude about Christmas, telling someone about Christ, etc.

PRAYER

Lead your family in a time of prayer expressing thanks for family and parents and children. Pray also that God would so prepare us for his coming that we would readily say yes to his call.

ASSIGNMENT

Ask everyone to do at least one thing that they know God is asking them to do.

DECEMBER **5**

Light Two Purple Candles

Preparing a Father

SCRIPTURE
READING

Matthew 1:18-25

MATERIALS
NEEDED

Something that symbolizes "Dad" in your family. If Dad is a golfer or tennis player, use some of his sports equipment. If he is in business, use something that is associated with his work. You may even want to use a picture of your own father holding you or sitting with you when you were a child. Children enjoy knowing that their parents were once children.

LESSON

Light two purple candles again. Remind everyone of this week's theme: preparation. Call on a family member to read the Scripture passage aloud.

   Hold up the object selected and explain why you think the object symbolizes Dad. Ask: "Why do you think fathers are important?" Allow everyone to express their ideas.

   After a few moments say something like, "God knew

that fathers were important too. Although God was Jesus' real father, Jesus would need an earthly 'stepfather.' God wanted to be sure that this would be a man who would raise Jesus in the right way. Do you think God made a good choice with Joseph? Let's see what was special about Joseph.

"First, the Bible says Joseph was a fair man [*just, righteous, principled*, 1:19]. That means he would treat all people the same. Joseph did not think some people were better than others.

"Also, Joseph was a caring person. At first he thought Mary was pregnant by another man. But even if that were true, he was not going to embarrass Mary or treat her badly. Instead Joseph decided to just quietly divorce her. This shows that Joseph was a caring person, sensitive to the feelings of others.

"Joseph was also a spiritual person. This means he was able to know when God was speaking to him. When the angel explained that God wanted the marriage to take place, Joseph knew in his heart that this was really God's word for him. Even though it did not seem possible, he was still willing to trust God.

"These three things together show that Joseph was a very special person. They help us understand why God chose him to be the one who along with Mary would take care of Jesus during his childhood.

"We can let our imaginations picture what a special love Joseph and Jesus must have had. As they worked together side by side in the carpenter shop, Joseph probably taught Jesus the importance of fairness, caring, and listening to God.

DISCUSSION "God prepared a special father for the job of taking care of young Jesus. God still prepares people for special work. What special work does he have for you? In what ways is he preparing you?" Spend time talking about God's work and preparation.

PRAYER Lead your family in prayer, asking God to prepare you and them for doing his work. Encourage them to also pray for the qualities of Joseph: fairness, compassion, and love for God.

ASSIGNMENT Encourage everyone to look for an opportunity to show kindness and/or forgiveness to someone tomorrow.

Preparing a Messenger

SCRIPTURE READING	Luke 1:5-17
MATERIALS NEEDED	A small radio.
LESSON	You won't have any trouble finding someone making an announcement or selling something as you turn the dial on the radio. As you find an example, start the lesson with an explanation of the role of an announcer.

Light two purple candles. Call on a family member to read the Scripture passage aloud. Turn on the radio to give everyone an example of what an announcer does. Ask about the announcer's role and work, why he/she is important, etc. Allow your children to express the work of the announcer in their own words.

Remind them of the news bulletins they gave a couple days ago. Then say something like, "God also prepared an announcer. He made sure that someone was ready to alert everyone that the new King was about to arrive. That announcer was John the Baptist.

"God took great care in preparing this special person. First of all, he started with John's parents, Zechariah and Elizabeth. They were faithful people who were waiting for the Messiah to come. They prayed daily that God's will would soon be done. They also longed for a child.

"Zechariah was a priest in the temple. His job was to pray that God would forgive the sins of Israel and save the people from punishment.

"Their child, who eventually became 'John the Baptist,' was destined to serve God's new King in an important way. The angel who spoke to Zechariah promised that his son would be a strong person with a clear sense of right and wrong. He would be a spiritual person, able to hear God's truth. He would also be a powerful preacher. He would care about people. He would want them to know that God's plan was about to be completed. He would urge them to turn away from sin and to believe the Good News that Jesus, the Messiah, was about to appear.

"John the Baptist was God's messenger, his announcer. John was the one prepared by God to announce that the waiting was over, the Good News was here, the Messiah had arrived.

DISCUSSION	"In our world there are people who do not know who Jesus is. Like John, we can tell others about Christ, preparing the way for his coming into their lives. God still prepares people to tell and hear the Good News." Ask how we can tell people about Christ today.
PRAYER	Pray together, thanking God for carefully preparing an announcer to proclaim the arrival of the King of kings. Thank God also for faithful servants who continue to announce the Good News. Ask God to prepare you to announce that Christmas is about the coming of our hope through Jesus Christ.
ASSIGNMENT	Ask everyone to make a Christmas card that would announce the coming of Jesus that they could send to a friend.

DECEMBER **7**

Light Two Purple Candles

Preparing the Great

SCRIPTURE
READING

Matthew 2:1-12

MATERIALS
NEEDED

Several different denominations of money—ones, fives, tens, and so forth. You will be using the pictures of the presidents as examples of great men.

LESSON

Light the first two purple candles again. Remind everyone of the theme for this week: preparation. Have everyone display the Christmas cards that they made. Have a family member read the Scripture passage aloud.

Pass around the bills. Ask: "Why are pictures of presidents on our money?" Allow children a few moments to come up with some answers. Guide them toward understanding that these were "great men." They played an important part in our history. We honor them by putting their pictures on our money.

Say something like, "Sometimes powerful people, like presidents or kings, find it difficult to obey God. Because they have power and influence over others, sometimes these leaders let themselves believe that they are even more powerful than God.

"That's what King Herod thought. He believed that if he could find the baby Jesus and kill him, he could stop God from raising up a new King. Herod was a powerful man, but he was not a great man. Truly great people recognize that their power and wisdom come from God.

"This is why the wise men (also called 'Magi,' and 'astrologers') are so important in the story of Jesus' birth. They were great men, with great wealth and power. Instead of fearing God's King and trying to kill him, however, they searched for him in order to worship him.

DISCUSSION

"These great men are powerful reminders that only in humble acceptance of God's gift do we really have the treasures of life. The wise men bowed themselves before the little King and offered him their worship. In doing so, they gave an important example of the way all of us must worship the Lord. In what ways can we worship Christ today?" Discuss this together.

PRAYER

Pray for all those leaders in the world who earnestly seek to be guided by the truth of God. Express thanks for truly great men and women who know that the only true power in the world exists in the grace of Jesus the Christ. As you anticipate the coming of the Lord, pray that God would prepare the great and the small to receive him.

ASSIGNMENT   Encourage everyone to look for an important person in the world who acknowledges Jesus as his or her Savior and Lord.

DECEMBER **8**

Light Two Purple Candles

Preparing the Humble

SCRIPTURE
READING

Luke 2:8-20

MATERIALS
NEEDED

A plate with a few crumbs of bread on it.

LESSON

Light the first two purple candles again. Have someone read aloud the Scripture passage for the day. Show the plate with a few bread crumbs to everyone. Ask: "How would you feel if you knew that this was going to be your only meal today?" Give everyone a chance to respond.

Then say something like, "The world is full of people who are poor, hungry, and alone. Many of them feel that no one cares for them. Some are deliberately punished by their governments simply for being poor. The poor in every land are almost always suspected to be potential criminals. People who live in alleys and sleep in cardboard boxes are avoided by people who live in houses.

"This kind of thing has always been true. At the time

Jesus was born, if a person could not get a job anywhere else, he might resort to being a shepherd. A shepherd was considered lowly and suspect.

"If we had lived in the days before Jesus was born, and someone had asked us, 'To whom do you think God will announce the arrival of his Messiah?' We would have named shepherds last, if we named them at all.

"And yet it is to shepherds that the angels came and announced the birth of the Savior. Those humble, poor, rejected persons were singled out by God for a special invitation to meet the new King. Why do you think God did that?" Allow time for everyone to answer.

"The poor and humble are accustomed to seeing prosperous and wealthy people pass them by as if they did not exist. If poor people had heard from the lips of townspeople that the new King had arrived, they would have immediately thought, *Well, the new King has come, but he will not care for us. We are the poor and the weak. What do we have for a king?*

"That's why God singled out the shepherds to be among the first witnesses to the coming of Jesus as Lord and Savior. In this way, God prepared the humble to understand this great truth: the gift of God's Son is for all kinds of people! High and low, weak and strong, rich and poor, male and female, slave and free—everyone is invited to meet the King and receive his blessing."

DISCUSSION "Who are the poor and humble people today? Where could we find them? What could we do to help them?" Discuss this for awhile.

PRAYER Thank God for remembering to prepare the way for the weak and the lowly. Pray also for those who even to this day have only crumbs for food.

ASSIGNMENT Have everyone imagine what it might feel like to be hungry. Write down how it feels. Option: Depending on when this lesson is done, perhaps dinner could be planned a half-hour later than usual and you could discuss your feelings of hunger and what truly hungry people must feel.

DECEMBER **9**

Light Two Purple Candles

Preparing the People

SCRIPTURE
READING

Luke 3:1-17

MATERIALS
NEEDED

If there are a few leaves on the ground around your house, pick some up. If possible, collect several different shades—brown, yellow, and so forth. One way to involve small children in the worship activities is to allow them to help you prepare. Invite little ones to help you pick some leaves. (You will probably end up with more than you need, but that's all right.) If leaves are not available, provide everyone with paper and crayons or colored pencils.

LESSON

Light two purple candles again. Briefly remind everyone of the theme for this second week of Advent. Ask a family member to read aloud the Scripture passage for the day. Call attention to the first part of verse 8. John's announcement that the new King was coming included a message for the people to "repent" and "bear the fruit of repentance." Ask what they think *repentance* means. Talk about this for awhile.

If leaves were gathered, show them to everyone. If leaves were not available, hand out paper and crayons and tell everyone to draw a spring leaf and an autumn leaf. (Very small children may need additional explanation and guidance.) Ask why the leaves are different colors. They came from the same tree, but at one point they were green, then yellow, then brown. Ask how something can change like that. Discuss this briefly.

DISCUSSION

"Can people change? I don't mean colors. Can people change the way they act, the way they think, the way they treat other people?" Allow everyone a few moments to consider the questions.

Then continue: "The answer is yes! People *can* change. And the word for change in people is the word that John the Baptist used to prepare the people for the coming of Jesus. He used the word *repent*.

"John also said that when people repent (that is, they change their mind about the way they are living), they will 'bear the fruit of repentance.' That means that the change of mind will cause people to act differently. Notice some of the changes that John mentioned:

• People having two coats would share with those having none;

• People having food would share with the hungry;

• Tax collectors would not force people to pay more than they really owe;

• Soldiers would not rob people or grumble at their superiors.

"In other words, John the Baptist prepared the people for the coming of Jesus the new King by telling them that they must change their minds, lives, and actions.

"God still does this important work. People are still able to 'repent,' to change and open their lives to the coming of Jesus. That is one reason we celebrate his coming. The birth of Jesus is God's way of changing our world for the better."

PRAYER

Ask God to help everyone change and become the kind of people he wants. Pray also that you and your family will be able to help others want to change so that their lives might be open to the coming of God's Son.

ASSIGNMENT

Ask everyone to decide on at least one thing they would like to change about themselves (attitude, habit, action, etc.). They should ask God to give them the power to make that change.

DECEMBER **10**

Light Two Purple Candles

Preparing Us

SCRIPTURE READING

John 17:20-26

MATERIALS NEEDED

A family portrait. If you do not have one, gather everyone together and pretend to be taking a family picture. Have some fun with this, adjusting hair, getting everyone to smile, and so forth.

LESSON

Light two purple candles again. Have a family member read the passage from John. This passage is a little difficult compared to some of the others, so you may want to read it or let another adult or older child tackle it. Have everyone note especially verses 21 and 22.

Show the family portrait or pretend to be taking one. Say something like, "One day our family will look different. You children will become adults. Possibly you will marry and have children. Try to imagine what *your* family portrait will look like. How many children will you have? Will they be boys or girls?" Discuss this briefly.

DISCUSSION

"Now, here are some really tough questions. How should parents help prepare their children for the future? How should they help their children get ready for adult life? How should they help children make decisions about jobs, education, and their own families? Questions about the future are difficult.

"In these verses, Jesus was praying about the future. He said, 'I'm not just praying for these' (that is, just the followers of his day), 'I am praying for those who believe in me through their word.' That means that Jesus was thinking about every person who would believe that he was the Savior. That's quite a lot to think about. What would Jesus' family portrait look like?" Discuss.

"How do you feel, knowing that Jesus was thinking about you before you were even born? Before any of us were even here, Jesus was making plans for our future. He was working in his life to make sure we would have life." Discuss.

"How do you think he prepared us?" Allow everyone to respond. Then say, "Jesus prepared us in many ways, through the Bible, the church, faithful workers, and teachers. All of these are part of a careful plan to help us meet the Lord. We are getting closer and closer to Christmas Day. We are feeling what it must have felt like to know that the new King was coming. Think of some ways God is preparing us to receive his Son."

PRAYER   Thank God for not overlooking anyone. Thank him for
                taking such special care in preparing people to see his Son
                and tell others about him. Also thank God for preparing a
                place in your hearts for his special gift.

ASSIGNMENT   Tell everyone to remember the time they accepted Christ
                as Savior. As they pray at bedtime, they should thank God
                for the people who prepared the way for them to meet
                Jesus.

A Week of Response
THIRD WEEK OF ADVENT
December 11 to December 17

Today nearly the whole world knows who Jesus is and about his coming to earth. The images of Bethlehem, a stable, and a manger are well known in our society. At the time these events were occurring, however, the news spread very slowly. In the beginning, only a handful of fortunate people witnessed the wonderful event.

How could this be? How could something that began as quietly as Jesus' birth become common knowledge to millions and millions of people? Part of the answer lies in how the eyewitnesses responded to what they saw. A few of those eyewitness accounts have become some of our most treasured stories. The eyewitnesses responded by telling everyone, and now the whole world knows. Such is the importance and power of a proper response.

Depending on the age of your children, you may need to take some time at the beginning of this week to help them understand what "response" means. This can be accomplished in a number of ways.

A good example is mail from a friend or relative. Explain to your children that when they receive a letter from someone, especially if that letter asks questions or requests information, a "response" is called for. We respond to the letter by sending a letter back.

Or you could have your children pretend they are schoolteachers. Ask what they would want children in their classes to do before they speak out or answer a question. (They will probably answer, "Raise a hand!") Raising the hand is part of a "response" to a question. Answering the question is also a form of response.

When you think your children have an idea of what "responding" means, you can point out that God has done much for us and has promised to give us many wonderful things. However, in order for these blessings to become ours, we must "respond." We respond to God by loving and trusting him.

The lessons for this week highlight several ways that special people responded to Jesus. We learn from these people some of the ways God wants us to respond to him today.

We light three purple candles during this week. The third purple candle is traditionally called the "Shepherds' candle." The lonely shepherds who responded with awe and joy typify a proper response to the coming of God in Christ Jesus.

FIFTEENTH DAY OF ADVENT

DECEMBER 11

Light Three Purple Candles

Responding with Thanksgiving

SCRIPTURE
READING

Luke 2:36-38

MATERIALS
NEEDED

Some printed thank-you cards. Thank-you notes that
you've recently received would be especially helpful. If you
don't have these, simply write on a sheet of paper in large
letters, "Thank You." Provide paper and pencils for everyone.

LESSON

Light three purple candles. Point out that today you are
lighting a new candle. It is called the Shepherds' candle,
and it stands for a proper response to God. (See the intro-
duction to this week's theme for suggestions in helping
children understand the meaning of *response*.) Explain
that you will see several important ways that people
responded to God's Son.

Call on a family member to read aloud the Scripture passage. Show everyone the thank-you cards or whatever you
have prepared. Ask: "Why is it important to say thank you

when someone does something for us?" Allow a few moments for everyone to think and respond.

Say something like, "When someone does something for us, we say thank you to let him or her know that we appreciate the act of kindness. We also let the person know that his or her kindness makes us feel special.

"The passage today tells a story of Anna, an elderly widow who felt that God had done something wonderful for her. She felt so strongly about it that she burst out in a prayer of thanksgiving right in the middle of the temple."

DISCUSSION

"What was she so thankful about?" (She knew that the baby Jesus was the promised Messiah.)

Continue: "Saying thank you to God is a proper response. When we realize how important the gift of his Son is to us, our hearts will be filled with thanks. Anna stayed in the temple night and day waiting for the new King. She knew that his coming would be the beginning of a new day for the whole world.

"If we can feel that way about the coming of Jesus, our lives will also be filled with thanksgiving." Ask: "How can we say thank you to God?"

PRAYER AND ASSIGNMENT

Have everyone think of some things for which they are thankful. Encourage everyone to think hard and decide how they might best say thank you to God. Suggest that everyone in the family write a thank-you note to God. Thank him for all of his care and love. Most of all, thank God for sending his Son to be the Savior.

Close the worship time with everyone working on their thank-you notes. Read them aloud as closing prayers.

DECEMBER **12**

Light Three Purple Candles

Responding with Obedience

SCRIPTURE
READING

Mark 1:16-20

MATERIALS
NEEDED

Thread a needle and have a piece of cloth on hand to demonstrate sewing.

LESSON

Light three purple candles again. Have a family member read aloud the Scripture passage for the day. Remind everyone that the theme for this week is "responding to God's gift."

Point out that when Jesus met Simon and Andrew, they were mending their fishing nets. Show the needle and thread. Demonstrate sewing by pushing the needle through the cloth and pulling it out on the other side. Explain that Simon and Andrew used a tool something like this needle and thread to repair their nets.

Call attention to the eye of the needle where the thread loops through. Say something like, "Notice that wherever the needle goes, the thread goes. It would be impossible to sew anything if the needle went one way and the thread another.

"The same thing is true of people who follow Jesus. Look at Simon and Andrew. They were busy working on their nets. Fishing was the way they made a living for their families. Jesus came and said, 'Follow me!' Just like a needle to thread. And what happened? The two men got up and immediately began following Jesus everywhere he went.

"That is obedience. When Jesus said, 'Come,' they obeyed. Later, when Jesus said, 'Go into all the world,' they obeyed again. Obedience is doing what God wants us to do. Obedience is like being thread—we follow the needle wherever it goes."

DISCUSSION

"What are some of the things God has told us to do?" Allow a little time for everyone to think and respond. Keep the process going by saying, "What else?" Encourage everyone to push beyond the usual things like: go to church, pray, tithe, and so forth.

Help children (and adults!) understand that obedience is a matter of relationship. Then continue by saying something like, "God expects us to love others, to love God with all our hearts, and to love our neighbors as ourselves.

"We are the thread. God will pull us and push us into all sorts of things. Jesus is the needle. We are attached to him.

When he leads, we respond with obedience and follow in his steps."

PRAYER   Ask God to help all of you become good and faithful followers. Pray also that you will be attached to Jesus like thread to a needle.

ASSIGNMENT   Encourage everyone to write down some of the ways God might lead us. Help children to think big (missions) and small (being kind to one another). Option for young children: Play the game Follow the Leader around the house or outside, with everyone getting a chance to lead.

DECEMBER **13**

Light Three Purple Candles

Responding with Prayer

SCRIPTURE
READING

Luke 2:25-33

MATERIALS
NEEDED

Bring a telephone to the area where you are using the Advent wreath. Most phones can be detached from their wall sockets. A cordless phone would work very well.

LESSON

Light three purple candles again. Ask someone to read Luke 2:25-33 aloud.

Hold up the phone and ask, "Who would you like to call tonight?" Children may suggest grandparents, school friends, and so forth. Adult family members should take part by also stating who they would like to call.

After a few moments, say something like, "A telephone is a wonderful invention because we can talk to people who are great distances away. We can hear their voices and they can hear us. We can tell loved ones we miss them, or tell them about things that are happening with us. We can also call for help or to get information.

"Wouldn't it be nice if we could call God on the phone? Every day we could call and ask for guidance. We could ask God what his will for us was for that day. We could get help with problems and answers to questions."

DISCUSSION

"Is there a way to talk to God?" Discuss briefly. Then say, "We can talk to God through prayer. Prayer is one of the proper responses to God's gift of Jesus our King.

"In our Scripture reading today, Simeon prayed immediately, as soon as he recognized that Jesus was the Messiah. Simeon prayed a prayer of thanksgiving (remember Anna?). He had waited a long time to see the fulfillment of God's promises.

"Simeon prayed for the success of Jesus' work. He knew that many hard days were ahead for Jesus and his followers. He also prayed for Mary and Joseph, Jesus' parents. He tried to prepare Mary as best as he could for the pain she would experience when her son gave his life.

"Simeon is a good example for us. When he met the Lord, he prayed. God wants us to pray too. The ability to open our hearts and minds to God in prayer is one way we can respond to his loving act of sending Jesus as Savior.

"Our prayers may take on many forms. We can pray for others. We can pray for our local church and pastor. We can pray for missionaries and other special workers. We can pray for people in trouble or in pain. The list is endless. This much is for sure. When we meet the promised King, God's Messiah, we are drawn to respond with prayer."

PRAYER   Pray together that as Christmas Day draws closer, you all will be ready to receive the wonderful blessing God has provided in his Son.

ASSIGNMENT   Encourage everyone to begin a prayer list. The names of friends or loved ones should be kept on the list. Any special needs in the family or community should also be kept on the list. Ask everyone to pray for the items on their list every day.

Responding with Patience

SCRIPTURE
READING

Luke 2:41-52

MATERIALS
NEEDED

A difficult jigsaw puzzle, perhaps one you have worked on as a family before. If a jigsaw puzzle is not available, a puzzle cube or triangle, crossword puzzle, objects hidden in a picture puzzle, or even a simple child's puzzle may be used.

LESSON

Light three purple candles again. Ask someone to read aloud the Scripture passage for the day. Display the object you have selected. Say something like, "This puzzle can be difficult to figure out. We could spend a long time trying to understand it. We would need a very special attitude in order to finish this puzzle. That attitude is called 'patience.'

"Patience means waiting while something that is not quite clear becomes clear. In the Scripture reading for today, Jesus' parents were confused and upset by Jesus' actions." Ask: "What did Jesus do to upset Mary and Joseph?" After a few answers, explain that Mary and

Joseph didn't lose their temper; they didn't scold or accuse Jesus. Instead they "patiently" asked him why he had stayed behind while the rest of the family went on."

Say: "Jesus' answer reveals that he was beginning to feel the urging of God in his life. His sense of purpose and mission was beginning to appear.

"Mary and Joseph knew their son was different. They also knew that God had chosen him for a very special purpose. They understood that there were things going on inside Jesus' head and heart that they could not understand. So Mary and Joseph did the only thing they could do—they responded by patiently waiting to see what would become of their son's life. They waited for the unclear to become clear. Their patience contributed to Jesus' growth 'in wisdom, and in years, and in favor with God and man' (2:52).

"Patience is also a proper response for us. We don't always understand what God is up to. Sometimes his will for us is unclear. We know who the Messiah is, but we don't always know where he is working and what he is trying to accomplish. We can know many things about God. But no one can know everything about God. Therefore, it is necessary for us to respond to God with patience. Many times we must simply wait for the unclear to become clear."

DISCUSSION   "When have you had to wait for God to give his answer, to make things clear?" Allow time for answers. "Why is it difficult to wait?"

Continue: "Life is much like a jigsaw puzzle. We are pretty sure the pieces fit together to form some kind of pattern. Sometimes they don't seem to fit very well. God has sent us his Son to help us figure the pieces out. We should be patient while working on the puzzle. God wants to make a beautiful pattern out of all of us."

PRAYER   Lead the family to pray for patience. Ask God to help you wait on him. Ask God also to help you all make the right decisions about your lives.

ASSIGNMENT   Ask everyone to list the things that require them to be patient and be ready to share them in tomorrow's lesson. Note: This would be a great time to set out a big jigsaw puzzle to be worked on over the holidays.

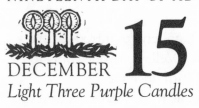

Responding with Recognition

SCRIPTURE READING

Mark 8:34-38

MATERIALS NEEDED

Small sheets of paper or index cards and enough straight pins or safety pins for everyone to have one. Self-adhesive labels will also work well. You will also need a magic marker or a crayon.

LESSON

Have everyone share their "patience lists" from yesterday's assignment. Light three purple candles again. Have a family member read aloud the Scripture verses for the day.

Pass out the slips of paper. Say something like, "At large meetings and conventions, people wear name tags so that everyone can know everyone else's name. Let's all write our names on our name tags and pin them to our shirts or blouses." Allow a few moments for everyone to make a name tag. Pin on your tag, but do not write your name on it; leave it blank.

After everyone has finished, pretend to introduce everyone using the name tags. Ask: "Well, is anyone going to introduce me? Why can't you introduce me?"

Say something like, "The same thing is true about Jesus. Before we can know Jesus, we must know his name. We must be able to recognize him and understand who he is. It is also impossible for us tell others who Jesus is unless we can recognize him. Recognition is part of our response to Jesus' coming into the world.

"In our Scripture reading today, Jesus asked his followers, 'Who do you think I am?' Peter said, 'You are the Christ, the Messiah, the promised King.'

"Jesus told Peter that he was right. Then Jesus said, 'I am going to die. I know you are not expecting this. You thought the King would be a great leader like King David. Well, you were wrong. I am going to suffer and die for my people. Don't be ashamed of me for this. That is what being the Savior is all about.'

"The followers of Jesus had trouble understanding this teaching. It took a long time before they really recognized what kind of king God had given them. Sometimes it is hard for us to recognize Jesus. Here are some ways we can know for sure we have seen the Messiah.

"We recognize Jesus when we understand why he came. Jesus came to help us. He was sent from God to give us new life. His obedience led him to a cross. That was part of

God's plan. God loved the world so much that he was willing to let his only Son die in our place.

"We recognize Jesus when we can see him at work in our world today. All around us God is at work. He is working through his people to help the poor and sick. He is working through his people to bring hope to hurting people everywhere. When we hear about people helping people, we can know that God is at work.

"We recognize Jesus when we try to live our lives according to his teachings. Jesus taught and lived in a way that pleased God. Our lives will also please God when we follow the example and teachings of Jesus.

"Finally, we recognize that Jesus is the promised King when we love him and trust him with our lives. When we are willing to say to the Lord, 'Here is my life, my gifts, my possessions, all that I have. Take them and use them,' then we can know we have recognized that Jesus is the promised King."

DISCUSSION   "Where have you seen Jesus recently? In whose life have you seen him at work?" Encourage everyone to give specific examples.

PRAYER   Ask God to help all of you know Christ when you see him. Pray also that other people may see the Lord in you.

ASSIGNMENT   Tell everyone to write down at least three specific times that they recognize Jesus in their lives or in others during the next 24 hours. They should be ready to tell these to the family next time.

Light Three Purple Candles

Responding with Faith

NOTE TO
PARENTS

Helping children develop a healthy understanding of the
meaning of *faith* is essential to their future religious and
spiritual growth. You may be part of an evangelical tradition that emphasizes conversion and the emergence of
faith as a gift from God. Or, you may be part of a liturgical
tradition and believe that faith is nurtured and bestowed
through the sacraments and the liturgy of the church.
Regardless of what sort of tradition you participate in,
defining *faith* and providing children with fairly concrete
examples of faith is enormously important. Adapt this
day's activity to conform to your understanding of the
nature of faith. The view offered grows out of an evangelical understanding.

SCRIPTURE
READING

Matthew 8:5-10

MATERIALS
NEEDED

A prescription medicine bottle.

LESSON

Have everyone share how they recognized Jesus, the assignment from the last lesson. Light three purple candles again. Have a family member read the Scripture passage for the day. Hold up the prescription medicine bottle. Ask: "Why do we go to the doctor and get medicine? Why don't we go to a car mechanic or to a plumber for medicine? How can we know that the medicine the doctor gives us is safe to take?" Discuss the questions for a few minutes. (Before moving on, small children should be reminded never to take medicines without a parent's supervision.)

Say something like, "We take the medicine because we have 'faith' in the doctor. We trust our doctor, and we believe that our doctor wants to help us get well. We believe that our doctor knows what he or she is doing.

"In our story from the Bible today, the Roman centurion was praised by Jesus for having faith. In fact, Jesus said that in all Israel he had not seen that kind of faith. The Roman soldier trusted Jesus. He believed that Jesus knew what he was doing. He believed that Jesus was God's special King. That is what faith is. And faith is part of the response God wants us to make to the coming of his Son.

"Faith has many parts. First of all, faith is trust. The centurion trusted Jesus with the health of his friend. He also trusted Jesus to do what he said he would do.

"Faith is respect. The centurion called Jesus 'Lord.' This

is a title of great honor. This powerful soldier would not have used this term unless he had great respect for Jesus.

"Finally, faith believes in God's power. The centurion knew that all Jesus had to do was say the word and his friend would be healed. We can also believe in God's power. God will help us and protect us. He will guide us and teach us. He will show us how we can grow. God will also help us when we try to serve him."

DISCUSSION   "Think of these three aspects of faith—trust, respect, and belief in God's power. In what ways can we show that we have faith in God?" Discuss this for a few minutes.

"Faith is an important response to God's gift of the new King. Faith opens the way for us to really know God and enjoy his blessings."

PRAYER   Lead the family in praying that God will help their faith grow and mature; help them to exercise their faith through prayer and worship; and help them use their faith to serve others.

ASSIGNMENT   Ask everyone to write out a definition of *faith* in their own words. Encourage family members to act on their own definition by being faithful.

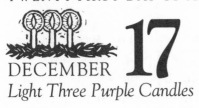

Light Three Purple Candles

Responding with Acceptance

SCRIPTURE
READING

Matthew 9:10-13

MATERIALS
NEEDED

If you have a copy of the children's story *The Ugly Duckling*, bring that to the worship time. If you do not have a copy, be prepared to tell the story. Better still, let the children tell *you* the story!

LESSON

Light three purple candles again. Have someone, selected in advance, read aloud the Scripture verses for the day. After the reading, introduce the story of *The Ugly Duckling*. Read the story or allow someone to tell the story. After the story ask: "How would you feel if no one cared for you? How would you feel if people made fun of you because of the way you looked or talked or dressed?" Allow a few moments for response.

Say something like, "It seems as though there are always some people who don't like other people. In Jesus' day, the Pharisees did not like tax collectors." (Note: For young children, explain in simple terms what Pharisees and tax collectors were.) "They called these people very bad names. The Pharisees also disliked people who did not worship the same way they did. They called these people 'sinners.' How do you think that made these people feel?" Discuss briefly.

Continue: "Jesus did not treat these people the way the Pharisees did. He made friends with them. He went to their homes and ate with their families. He treated them with kindness and respect.

"The Pharisees were angry with Jesus. They did not think he should go to the homes of these people. They began calling Jesus names. Jesus reminded the Pharisees that the prophets had said that God wanted mercy, not fancy worship services. In other words, Jesus thought it was more important to treat people right than it was to dress right and do all the right things in church.

DISCUSSION

"This is still true. There are a lot of people in our world today who are unloved." Ask: "Who are some people that you know who are not liked very much? Who do you know who are called names?" Allow time for everyone to respond.

Say: "When God sent his Son into the world, one of his purposes was to bring people together—to teach us how to love others. Part of our response to the coming of Jesus as King is to treat people the same way he did.

"The reasons for doing this are important. If we don't accept people and treat them with respect, they might get the idea that God does not want them either. Think how sad people would be if they went through life believing God did not love them.

"Remember the ugly duckling? He turned out to be a beautiful swan. The people in our world who seem ugly or mean might just be the same way. Given a chance, they might turn out beautiful. Maybe all they need is for someone to accept them and love them. Think about someone you know who needs to be accepted, respected, and loved."

PRAYER

Lead the family in praying for the unloved people in our world—the poor, the homeless, the tired, the aged, the lonely, and many others. Ask God to guide you to people in your town or community who may feel unwanted.

ASSIGNMENT

Explain to the family that when God guides them to people who need love, they should show people the same love and acceptance as Jesus did to the tax collectors and sinners. Tell them to send a Christmas card to someone they know who gets picked on a lot or who may be lonely or hurting.

Celebrating
the Love of God
FOURTH WEEK OF ADVENT
December 18 to December 24

The word *love* carries a great deal of weight in our language. The same word is applied to pizza, puppies, cars, trees, hunting, golf, wives, and children. Hopefully, we don't mean the same thing every time.

When we use the word properly, we are trying to express our deepest emotions about something. Love, at its best, is the height of human affection and loyalty. We have learned to understand that God is love. In sending Jesus as the Messiah, love became a person.

We can think about God's love in two ways. First, love is a motive. God's love is his motive for his gracious acts. Because God loves the world so much, he sent his Son to save it. In the love of God we find hope, mercy, forgiveness, and reconciliation.

But God's love can also be understood as our motivation. We should love because God first loved us. Jesus commanded us: "Be perfect as your father in heaven is perfect. . . ." The context of that command is love (Matthew 5:43-48). In other words, not only does God's love create the ground for our salvation and hope, but God's love also becomes the example for our own love.

This final week of Advent concentrates on this love—God's love moving toward us and God's love flowing from us. We light a pink candle this week called the "Love candle." This brighter, lighter colored candle symbolizes the effects of God's love. The darkness begins to give way under the impact of God's gracious acts.

You have the opportunity to lead your family to appreciate the power and importance of this central biblical truth.

DECEMBER **18**

Light Three Purple Candles and One Pink Candle

Love Casts Out Fear

SCRIPTURE
READING

1 John 4:16-21

MATERIALS
NEEDED

A small nightlight.

LESSON

Light the four candles. Point out that for the first time in your Advent celebration you have a candle of a different color. This pink candle stands for God's love. It is a lighter color than the others because it represents the hope and happiness that God's love provides.

Read aloud the Scripture passage from 1 John. If you have children old enough, allow one of them to read. Point out verse 18 that states, "Perfect love casts out fear." Tell everyone that the word *perfect* means "grown-up," "fully developed," or "mature."

Hold up the nightlight. Say something like, "Some people are afraid of the dark. They cannot rest at night if their house is completely without light; therefore, they place small lights like this one in outlets around the house to drive the darkness away. As long as they can see through the darkness, they are not afraid.

"Our love for God does the same thing. When we have a love for God that is "mature" or "fully developed," we find that we don't have to be afraid of scary things in the world. And we can do everything that God wants us to do that seems frightening and difficult."

Ask the children to name some of the things they are afraid of. (They might mention darkness, strangers, snakes, loud noises, and so on.) Name some of the things that you are afraid of. (You might include some of the items from the children's list.) Say: "Sometimes fear is good. When we see a snake or approach a busy intersection, fear helps us to be careful. But sometimes the things we are afraid of are just in our minds. Imaginary fears can keep us from being happy and growing the way God would like us to." (Use an appropriate example from your list or the children's. Fear of the dark may be an example.)

"As we grow in our love for God, many of our imaginary fears go away. The stronger our love for God becomes, the more we will be able to understand that he does not want us to hide from the world." (Be sensitive to special needs. For example, your child may express a fear of death. This will provide a good opportunity to demonstrate how our loving God can help us face the prospect of our own death.)

"God's gift of love entered the world in the dark but was marked by a huge nightlight in the sky. God split the darkness, and he invites us not to be afraid. The candles burning on our wreath remind us that perfect love casts out fear."

DISCUSSION

"How can knowing that God loves us and is with us help us when we're afraid?" Take time to discuss how Christians should react in a fearful situation.

PRAYER

Lead your family to pray, thanking God for his care and protection. Ask the Lord to help all of you to "grow up" in your love for him and for each other.

ASSIGNMENT

Give everyone an index card and a pen. Then read the following verses aloud, one at a time: Psalm 27:1; Proverbs 29:25; Mark 6:50; 1 John 4:18a. Tell them each to choose one verse and write it out on the card. They should put these cards in a place where they will see them often (such as on a bulletin board, on a mirror, next to the bed, in a Bible, etc.).

DECEMBER **19**

Light Three Purple Candles and One Pink Candle

Love Has No Enemies

SPECIAL NOTE

You may have relatives serving in the armed forces. Jesus' teachings about "loving enemies" will be very difficult to hear if our servicemen and women are involved in fighting. Of course, the ideals of God's kingdom have always challenged us.

While being sensitive to the special circumstances an armed conflict creates for families, it is nevertheless important to assert God's vision for us. His expectations always transcend our national and economic interests.

Jesus' intent is not to condone the evil actions of humans. He wants to challenge us not to sink to the level of hate and vengeance in our efforts to stop evil. Stop evil we must! But if we come to resemble our opponent in the process, then evil simply changes sides. On the other hand, if we restrain evil and hate evil deeds without hating the perpetrators, we will approach the ideal that Jesus outlines in the passage for this day's activity.

As Jesus was being nailed to his cross he prayed, "Father forgive them, they don't know what they are doing." We still don't know what we're doing, and we find it difficult to forgive others. Forgiveness and love, therefore, continue to be relevant lessons for us to learn. Today's activity is aimed at accomplishing that goal.

SCRIPTURE READING	Matthew 5:43-48
MATERIALS NEEDED	None.
LESSON	Light the three purple candles and one pink one. Remind everyone that this is the week of love. We celebrate God's love moving toward us in Jesus. We also celebrate God's love moving through us toward others. Have a family member read the Scripture passage for the day.

Invite everyone to name some enemies. Present or past national conflicts may be appropriate. Children may need some definition concerning who an enemy is. (Isn't it an interesting irony that children must be taught what an enemy is!) Children may name a schoolmate.

Ask, "Is it hard or easy to like people who like us? Is it hard or easy to be nice to people who do nice things for us?" Allow everyone a chance to respond. Then ask, "Is it |

hard or easy to like people who *don't* like us? How about people who are mean to us or hurt us—is it hard or easy to like them?" Discuss this briefly.

Say something like, "Jesus teaches that because we are children of God we should imitate God. One of the things God does is love his enemies. Why does God love people who do not love him? Here are several reasons:

1. *God gives hope*. If God turned against his enemies, they would have no hope. By loving these people, God provides a way for them to become his friends. As long as God loves them, there is a chance that they will change for the better.

2. *God is patient*. He is willing to wait and see if people will change. God knows that sometimes we do things, wrong things, because we don't know any better. Sometimes people are hateful because they have been hurt themselves. God is willing to wait and see if people will respond to kindness and love.

3. *God is love*. It is not in God's nature to hate people. Even when he punishes his children, it is not out of hate but out of love. When God corrects us, it is because he wants to help us, not destroy us. Parents do the same thing. When we discipline our children, it is because we love them.

DISCUSSION

"The only hope that some people have of being free from their mean and hateful lives is to discover that God loves them. How do you think that might happen? Well, that is where we come in. Discuss how everyone can tell others about God's love.

"If we imitate God and love our enemies, we become constant reminders that God cares for people. He cares for them even when they do evil things. When we choose to hate our enemies and treat them as badly as they treat us, we are not showing how God feels. We are really imitating our enemy instead of our God. By following God's example and loving those who do not love us, we show the world what God's love looks like.

"Remember this, it was a dark world, a world filled with hate and violence, into which God sent his Son. That Son, Jesus, was given to remind all of us that God loves all people, even those who do not love him back.

"It is difficult to love enemies, but God will help us. And when we succeed at that, we can know that we are as close to God as a person can be."

PRAYER AND ASSIGNMENT

Ask everyone to rename the persons they identified as enemies at the beginning of the lesson. Lead your family in prayer for these people. Ask God to help you love your enemies. This does not mean that you look the other way when they do evil things. It simply means that no matter what they do, you will treat them as persons and work for their redemption. In other words, loving your enemies means treating them exactly the way God has treated you. Actually, love has no enemies. Tell them to continue to pray for their enemies.

DECEMBER **20**

Light Three Purple Candles and One Pink Candle

Love Is Generous

SCRIPTURE
READING

Mark 6:34-44

MATERIALS
NEEDED

A plate of cookies or crackers. Make sure there are two cookies for everyone except you. (For example, if there are four people in your family, you should have six cookies or crackers.) Leave plenty of crumbs on the plate. If necessary, take a separate cookie or cracker and crumble it up. Then scatter a few of the crumbs around the plate. Lay the whole cookies or crackers on top of the crumbs.

LESSON

Have a family member light the three purple candles and one pink candle on the Advent wreath. Remind everyone of the theme for the week and that the pink candle symbolizes God's love. Read the Scripture passage aloud.

Pass around the plate of cookies and crackers. Tell everyone to take two but not to eat them yet! After you have given all the cookies say, "Uh-oh, there aren't any cookies left for me. Well, I guess I just get the crumbs!"

"How would you feel if you knew there was plenty of food in the house, but all we ever gave you were crumbs?" Allow everyone a chance to imagine how they would feel. Encourage creative responses. Then ask: "Are there hungry people in our world?" (Yes. There is a great deal of hunger in our world.) "Where?" Discuss this for awhile.

Then say something like, "In the Scripture passage we read, Jesus was surrounded by hungry people. His disciples wanted to send them away. They did not want to have to deal with the people's hunger. But Jesus told them, 'You give them something to eat!' (6:37). They took what they had, which was not very much, and gave it to Jesus. He blessed it and multiplied it and fed everyone there.

"You see, love is generous. When we love people, we are concerned about their well-being. If people are hungry and we love them, we will want to help them. But how? The same way the disciples did. They shared what they had with the hungry crowd. Jesus made it enough.

"Each of you has two cookies. I have none. What can you do to help me have food? If you give me all your cookies, then you will have none. That's not a good plan. Suppose you broke your cookies in half and each of you gave me half a cookie?" (Let everyone do that.) Now we all have enough. All of us have some because you were generous and shared with me."

DISCUSSION "We can help hungry people in the world in the same way. We have more than we need. We can share, and God will bless it and multiply it." Ask: "What can we do this week to help someone who is hungry?" Discuss this for a few minutes.

PRAYER Lead your family in a prayer of thanksgiving for the rich ways that God has blessed you. Pray also for the unfortunate persons of the world who are hungry every day of their lives. Ask God to help your love express itself in acts of generous sharing. Ask the Lord to take your offerings and bless them and multiply them to meet the needs of the needy.

ASSIGNMENT Look for one way to share the Lord's blessings with another person and do it.

Note: You may want to choose a family project (such as sponsoring a child through a Christian social agency, helping at a food pantry, collecting food for the needy, etc.).

DECEMBER 21

Light Three Purple Candles and One Pink Candle

Love Is Kind

SCRIPTURE
READING

Luke 10:30-37

MATERIALS
NEEDED

An old towel or T-shirt tied as a sling for you to put your arm in.

LESSON

Light the three purple candles and one pink candle again. Ask for a volunteer to explain what the pink candle stands for. Have a family member read aloud the Scripture passage for the day.

Put your arm in the sling and pretend to walk with a limp. Moan a little just for dramatic effect! Ask: "How would you feel if I was injured and could not get around very well? Would you help me? Would you take care of me?" Allow everyone a chance to express their feelings.

Then ask, "Why would you take care of me? Because you love me?" Give strong affirmation to everyone's positive response.

Say something like, "That is very good. One of the

things that is true about love is that love is kind. That is what Jesus was getting at in his story of the Good Samaritan. There are three examples of unkindness in Jesus' story. What are they?" (The robbers, the priest, and the Levite.)

"We don't expect robbers to be kind, but we do expect God's people to be kind. In Jesus' story, the people who should have helped the poor, beaten man ignored him and went on their way. That is not love.

"Only one person in Jesus' story did the loving thing. Who was that?" (The Samaritan.) "Now look what Jesus says we should do. He is talking about the Samaritan man, and he says: 'Go and do the same thing!' In other words, we can show the love of God in us by loving people who are hurt or are in need.

DISCUSSION

"Yesterday we talked about hungry people. What other kinds of people are hurt and in trouble?" Allow everyone a few moments to think and respond. Encourage creative thinking. Children may mention friends who are in trouble in school or whose families are having severe problems. Adults might mention friends who have lost their jobs or who have a serious illness.

After a few minutes of discussion ask: "If love is kind, how can we show love to the people we know who are in trouble?" (Possible answers will include: We can pray for them. We can tell them we care for them. We can offer our friendship.) If that's all they say, ask: "What else?" (Other answers could include: We can listen when they need to talk. We might help them with their schoolwork or invite them to our house for a meal.) Help them see specific, concrete ways that they can help hurting people.

"Love is kind. When we love people and show them we love them through acts of kindness, we also are showing them God's love. Sharing God's love is what Christmas is all about."

PRAYER

Lead your family in prayer for any friend whose name may have come up as being in need. Ask God to show you a way to help that person through some act of kindness.

ASSIGNMENT

Brainstorm specific ways that each of you can help a friend.

DECEMBER **22**

Light Three Purple Candles and One Pink Candle

Love Never Fails

SCRIPTURE
READING

1 Corinthians 13:1-8

MATERIALS
NEEDED

A piece of string or thread that can be easily broken.

LESSON

Have a family member light the three purple candles and one pink candle on the Advent wreath. Have someone read aloud the Scripture passage for the day.

   Note: The King James Version uses the word *charity* where most modern translations use the word *love*. If you are using the KJV, you will probably need to take a minute and explain the word. Also, at verse 8, which is the focal verse for this activity, some translations say, "Love never ends." The Greek word used here literally means "fail." The meaning seems slanted more to the success or effectiveness of love rather than love's duration. The lesson for today is based on the idea that God's love does not quit or give up.

Hold up the string that you have brought with you. Say something like, "This is an unbreakable string. It said so on the package. Watch what happens when I pull on it." (Give it a good yank. Of course, it will break.) Continue: "Oh my! I guess this is not unbreakable string after all. This string failed. It could not do what it claimed it could do.

"In our Bible reading we find that God's love is supposed to be unbreakable. The words used are: 'Love never fails!' Other things in life might fail, but not God's love. God has promised us that his love is unbreakable. Whatever he sets his love to do, his love will do!

"Let's see if we can think of some things God's love has done." Allow children a chance to respond to each question.

"God's love wanted to bring the children of Israel out of Egypt. Did his love succeed?

"As we saw earlier in this book, God wanted to bring his people out of Babylon and restore them to their homes. Did his love succeed?

"God wanted the whole world to know about his love. He wanted to give the world a special gift that would show his love. God wanted the world to know how far he was willing to go to make his love available. Did he do all those things? How?" (By sending Jesus into the world.)

Recite John 3:16 together: "For God so loved the world

that he gave his only Son, that whoever believes in him should not perish but have eternal life" (RSV).

Continue: "God's love never fails. He does not quit or give up on us. He works diligently to bring us into his presence and into his will. God's love will never let us down.

"There is one more thing we need to say about God's love. Once we receive God's love, God wants us to share it. He wants us to let his love touch other people through us. Our challenge is for the unfailing love of God to be active in our lives. In other words, we should try to love others without failing. We are not perfect as God is perfect—sometimes we will fail to love others as we should. But our goal should be to keep trying."

DISCUSSION "How can we let God's love touch others through us?" Discuss this for a few minutes.

PRAYER Thank God for the gift of love in his Son. Ask God to help you all live in such a way that the unfailing love that saves you will also touch the lives of others through you.

ASSIGNMENT Tell everyone to decide on two people to whom they can show God's unfailing love. Then they should do a loving act for each person in the next few days.

DECEMBER 23

Light Three Purple Candles and One Pink Candle

Love Creates Hope

SCRIPTURE
READING

Mark 2:1-12

MATERIALS
NEEDED

Learn the following story and be able to tell it with enthusiasm.

Once upon a time, two frogs fell into a vat of cream. The walls of the vat were too high for the frogs to jump out. For a long time they swam around in the cream trying to figure out what to do. They seemed to be trapped.

Finally, one of the frogs said, "This is hopeless. There is no way out of this. We will be stuck here like this forever. I'm giving up." With that the frog quit swimming, sank to the bottom of the vat, and drowned.

The other frog said to himself, "I will not lose hope. There must be a way out of here. I'm going to keep swimming in this cream until I find a way." And he kept swimming.

In fact, he swam so much and so hard that the cream began to change. The frog did not know it, but when cream is stirred long enough and hard enough, it turns into butter. That frog kept swimming around until the cream finally turned into butter. With a good solid floor of butter under him, he easily hopped out.

It is very important for all of us never to lose hope. No matter how difficult things may seem, there is always a way out or through.

In preparation, read over the story several times. You may even want to simulate the "swimming" motions of the frogs just for dramatic effect.

LESSON

Light the three purple candles and one pink one again. Have a family member read aloud the Scripture passage for the day.

Begin by saying, "Let me tell you an interesting story." Then tell the frog story with feeling. Afterward, ask everyone to explain in their own words what they think *hope* means. Little ones may need some additional clarification. Refer to the story for illustrations.

After everyone has expressed a view, say: "One of the reasons that God sent Jesus into the world was to give us hope. God knows that at times life can be very difficult. If we do not have hope, we will become like the frog who sank to the bottom.

"Our Scripture reading is another good example. There was a man who had never walked in his whole life. Can you imagine how he must have felt as a child? Every day all of his friends, brothers, and sisters would go outside to run and play, but he was trapped.

"How do you think he felt when four of his friends came to take him to Jesus? What do you think he said? He may have answered: 'Oh, I don't want to go. There is nothing anyone can do for me. I've been this way all my life. I'll never be any different. There is no way out of this trap I'm in. Just leave me alone!' He could have sounded like our frog friend that drowned.

"Or, he could have said this: 'Do you really think Jesus can help me? Well, it's worth a try. Will you fellows help me? Will you carry me to Jesus?'

"We can't know for sure how the paralyzed man reacted to the idea. We can know for sure what happened to his life. Through Jesus, this man found a way out of his sad situation.

"When God sent Jesus into the world, he was saying to us loud and clear: 'Don't give up! There's hope for you! Don't quit swimming, don't quit trying, don't give up on yourself!'

"With Jesus, there is always a way out of our trouble. The love of God creates hope for us. And from time to time, we need hope to get us through."

DISCUSSION

"In what situations do you lose hope or feel like giving up? How can God's love create hope in you?" Discuss these questions for awhile.

PRAYER   Thank God for the hope that is Jesus. Pray that you will
                        live in hope. Pray that you will not give up on yourselves
                        no matter how difficult things may become. With God,
                        there is always a way!

ASSIGNMENT   Tell everyone to make an acrostic with the letters H-O-P-E
                        or L-O-V-E. They should list a series of words, each one
                        beginning with the appropriate letter, that relate to hope
                        and/or love. For example:

                            Long; God's love never ends
                            Open; God's love is for everyone
                            Victorious; God's love always wins
                            Everywhere; God's love is all around us

                            OR

                            God's love
                            Has
                            Only
                            Perfect
                            Effects!

                        They should be prepared to give their acrostics next
                        time. Note: Team very young children with older children
                        or parents.

DECEMBER **24**

Light Three Purple Candles and One Pink Candle

Love, the Greatest Gift

SCRIPTURE
READING

1 Corinthians 13:8-13

MATERIALS
NEEDED

By now, you probably have some presents under the tree. Use one of them for this activity. If presents are not out in your house until Christmas morning, take a small box and wrap it in some Christmas paper. What you are looking for is something to stimulate thinking about "gifts."

LESSON

Light the three purple candles and one pink candle again. Have a family member read aloud the Scripture passage for today.

Show everyone the "present" you have brought with you. Ask: "What was the best present you ever received? What made it special to you?" Allow everyone a chance to respond. Be sure to encourage answers to both questions, and don't forget to take part yourself.

After everyone has described his/her favorite gift say: "Now, what do you think is the greatest gift God ever gave to us? That's easy. God's greatest gift is his Son. That is what Christmas is all about. We are celebrating God's gift of his Son." Ask, "Why did God send his Son?" Allow time for answers. Then say: "God sent Jesus to us because he loves us. Part of the greatest gift in the world then is love. The passage we just read makes a real point of that. There are many things in life that are important. Name some really important things in life." (Help children to expand their thinking. Answers might include parents, school, grades, friends, pets, grandparents, church, possessions, and so forth.)

Affirm all answers. Say, "These are all important, and, in a way, they are gifts from God. But the most important is love. Why?" After everyone has had a chance to answer, present the following points:

1. *Love rescues us from selfishness.* If we only think about ourselves all the time, we are not going to be very loving people.

2. *Love helps us to see hurting people in our world.* The only way that people in need can be helped is for other people to help them. God sends his blessing through us. Love helps us see the need.

3. *Love helps us to understand things.* In our Scripture passage it says, "Right now it's like looking into a dim mirror." Sometimes life is not very clear. Sometimes it doesn't

make sense. The Bible says that love helps us figure things out."

DISCUSSION "If you could give every person in the world the most special gift anyone could have, what would it be? If you say the gift of God's love, you are right. It is the one thing we all need."

PRAYER Say something like, "Tomorrow is Jesus' birthday. It is a day of gift-giving and happiness. Let's pray tonight, as we look forward to the nice presents we will get and give tomorrow, that God will use us to help give the greatest gift of all. The gift of his love in Jesus." Then lead the family in prayer, with each person expressing thanks to God for his gift of Jesus.

ASSIGNMENT Encourage everyone to prepare a small, special gift for the other members of the family. This should be something personal and handmade. This gift could be a poem or a note. Give these presents first in the morning.

DECEMBER **25**

Light All Five Candles!

The King Dressed in Rags

NOTE

Christmas Day is likely to be full of activities. Plan carefully for a time when your Advent celebration can be brought to an appropriate close. While the children are looking at unopened presents under the tree is probably not a good time. If you have been meeting during the evening, use that same time. This closing activity will allow you an opportunity to lead your family to reflect on the meaning of the day.

SCRIPTURE
READING

Luke 2:1-7

MATERIALS
NEEDED

Cut up some old cleaning rags. If your children are recently out of diapers and you have some that you use for cleaning or dusting, these would be very effective. If old diapers are not available, then use a tattered shirt, towel, or dish cloth—anything that you would consider "rags."

LESSON

Light all five candles on the Advent wreath. Point out the central white candle. Explain that this candle is the Christ candle. His white candle is brighter because he is the light of the world! Our hope, our life, our King and our Savior has finally come!

Have a family member read aloud the Scripture passage. Call everyone's attention to the statement that Jesus was wrapped in swaddling clothes (or cloths, blanket, etc., depending on the translation you use) (2:7).

Show everyone the rags. Say something like, "The Bible tells us that Jesus was wrapped in 'swaddling clothes.' This is a very important piece of information. It tells us something about the newborn King. Swaddling clothes literally means 'the rags of the poor.' Why do you think God allowed Jesus to be born to poor parents?" Allow a few moments for response.

Say: "If Jesus had been born in a palace, he would have been wrapped in fine linen and silk. But he was not born to rich parents. Jesus was born into a home that could only afford 'rags' for diapers and blankets.

"God sent Jesus to everyone. If Jesus had been born to rich parents or raised in a king's house, ordinary people would have difficulty reaching out to him. Therefore, God sent Jesus to poor people. The King, the Messiah, was born to a family who could only afford rags to wrap him in.

"But that means that all kinds of people can reach out to

Jesus. Rich people, poor people, weak people, powerful people—all people can come to Jesus and receive his blessing.

"Think about the special people that God prepared to introduce his Son to the world. Remember the shepherds who saw the angels? They were poor and needy. Yet they came and bowed before the newborn King. Remember the wise men? They were rich and powerful. Yet they also came and bowed themselves before the child Jesus.

"That is one reason God sent his Son into the world through a poor family. The Bible says that 'he humbled himself and became an obedient servant' (Philippians 2:6-7). Anyone can draw near to this special king. Anyone!

"There is another reason for Jesus coming into the world wrapped in rags. It is to remind us where our real hope is. The hope for our world is not in the gathering of wealth and fine things. The hope for our world is not in the hands of powerful leaders, kings, or rulers. The hope for our world is not in the gold and fine jewels of the palaces of this world. Our hope for this world is in Jesus Christ, God's Son.

"In a way, we are all poor and in need. Without Jesus our lives do not work the way they should. We walk in darkness and despair. We do things that hurt us and others. We put our trust in things that take life away from us instead of giving life to us. Many people live in hate and violence.

"This is why we celebrate Christmas. It is not just the birth of Jesus that is important. The birth was just the beginning. We celebrate the gift of life and hope. We light candles because God has split the darkness. We give gifts because God has given his Son to us. We do acts of love and kindness because God has poured his love out on us.

"God carefully prepared a world to receive his Son. That Son was sent to us as a gift—a gift wrapped in the rags of poverty. Jesus' life, his teachings, his love, and ultimately his death, were all gifts from God. These gifts were given to show us a way out—a way out of our darkness, out of death and despair, out of hate and violence.

"Our only hope is to follow him."

DISCUSSION

"For Christians, Christmas is not an ending but a beginning." Ask them to each share one way they can celebrate Christmas every day of the year!

PRAYER

Lead your family in a prayer of commitment. Ask the Lord of grace and mercy to help you follow the lead of the new King. Pray, acknowledging that Jesus is Lord as well as Savior of your lives. Pray, asking God to help you follow a King born in a stable and wrapped in the rags of the poor.

ASSIGNMENT

Have everyone think of one person with whom they can share the real meaning of Christmas.